Pomeranian

Series "Fun Facts on Dogs for Kids"

Written by Michelle Hawkins

Pomeranian

Series "Fun Facts on Dogs for Kids"

By: Michelle Hawkins

Version 1.1 ~February 2021

Published by Michelle Hawkins at KDP

Copyright ©2021 by Michelle Hawkins. All rights reserved.

No part of this publication may be reproduced, distributed or transmitted in any form or by any means including photocopying, recording or other electronic or mechanical methods or by any information storage or retrieval system without the prior written permission of the publishers, except in the case of very brief quotations embodied in critical reviews and certain other noncommercial uses permitted by copyright law.

All rights reserved, including the right of reproduction in whole or in part in any form.

All information in this book has been carefully researched and checked for factual accuracy. However, the author and publisher make no warranty, express or implied, that the information contained herein is appropriate for every individual, situation, or purpose and assume no responsibility for errors or omissions.

The reader assumes the risk and full responsibility for all actions. The author will not be held responsible for any loss or damage, whether consequential, incidental, special or otherwise, that may result from the information presented in this book.

All images are free for use or purchased from stock photo sites or royalty-free for commercial use. I have relied on my own observations as well as many different sources for this book, and I have done my best to check facts and give credit where it is due. In the event that any material is used without proper permission, please contact me so that the oversight can be corrected.

Two Pomeranians survived the sinking of the Titanic out of twelve dogs.

Pomeranians are not very popular in the United Kingdom and Australia.

Houdini had a Pomeranian.

The average age of a Pomeranian is between twelve and sixteen years of age.

Pomeranians are considered a toy breed.

Other names for Pomeranians are Pommy, Pom Pom, Pom, Teddy Bear, and Foxy Dog.

Pomeranians are part of the spitz family/breed.

Pomeranians need daily playtime.

Pomeranians are very lightweight.

The American Kennel Club accepts eighteen different colors of Pomeranians.

Pomeranians must have attention.

The tail on a Pomeranian should not curl.

Pomeranians are loyal companions.

Pomeranians crave lots of attention.

When training Pomeranians, training must be consistent.

The most famous Pomeranian is named Boo on Facebook.

Brush your Pomeranian often so that they will shed less.

Pomeranians are very attentive to their owner.

Pomeranians have a total of twenty-three different colors.

Pomeranians are a very sturdy dog breed.

In 1988 a Pomeranian became best in show.

The original Pomeranians were double the size they are today.

Pomeranians are great with children.

Pomeranians are cuddle bugs with their owner.

Pomeranians are very affectionate.

Pomeranians are considered a small toy breed.

Pomeranians are good at reading the emotions of their owner.

Queen Victoria had a Pomeranian.

Pomeranians are one owner dogs.

For seniors, Pomeranians would make a good companion.

Pomeranians have a double coat.

The coat on a Pomeranian needs to be trimmed every other month.

If left alone, Pomeranians can have separation anxiety.

Pomeranians make good watchdogs.

Pomeranians are a relative health breed.

Families with older children, Pomeranians make great pets.

As Pomeranians age, their fur can change colors.

Pomeranians are loyal.

Pomeranians are small and compact.

Pomeranians are an inside dog.

Pomeranians are good therapy dogs.

Pomeranians need a little exercise.

Pomeranians are very intelligent.

Pomeranians came from the Pomeranian region of Europe.

The teeth of a Pomeranian needs to be brushed at least twice a week.

Pomeranians are energetic.

Pomeranians are easy to travel with.

Pomeranians do not drool.

Pomeranians have a fluffy tail.

Pomeranians were accepted into the American Kennel Club in 1898.

The female Pomeranians are bigger than the males.

Pomeranians make a good watchdog.

Pomeranians are great for apartment living.

Pomeranians are protective of their owners.

Pomeranians need to learn the command quite very early on.

Pomeranians are easy to train.

The most common colors of a Pomeranian is black, cream, orange, or white.

When a Pomeranian's nose is cold, they will use their tail to keep it warm.

Pomeranians can be very mischievous.

Due to their small mouth, Pomeranians can have teeth crowding.

When Michelangelo painted the Sistine Chapel, his Pomeranian kept him company on a satin pillow.

When happy or excited, Pomeranians will spin in circles.

The fur on a Pomeranian is very thick.

Pomeranians love attention from everyone.

Sir Isacc Newtons Pomeranian enjoyed chewing on his manuscripts.

President Teddy Roosevelt owned a Pomeranian.

Pomeranians are one of the top fifteen registered American Kennel Breeds.

Pomeranians have a very yappy bark.

Pomeranians have pointed ears.

The average size of a litter of puppies for a Pomeranian is between two to three puppies.

Pomeranians can have food allergies.

Pomeranians have a very high pitched bark.

Pomeranians are in the top twenty of the most popular dogs in the American Kennel Club.

Pomeranians eat very little.

Pomeranians are related to Huskies and Akitas.

When you brush Pomeranians, make sure you are brushing upward.

A daily walk of twenty to thirty minutes is ideal.

The fur on a Pomeranian is very soft.

Pomeranians have been around since as early as the sixteenth century.

Pomeranians are quick learners.

Pomeranians are very obedient.

The average weight of a Pomeranian is between three to seven pounds.

Pomeranians can have many different haircuts.

The fur on a Pomeranian is very bright.

At one year, Pomeranians are considered fully grown.

Pomeranians are suitable for older children, but not for younger children.

Find me on Amazon at:

https://amzn.to/3oqoXoG

and on Facebook at:

https://bit.ly/3ovFJ5V

Other Books by Michelle Hawkins

Series

Fun Facts on Birds for Kids.

Fun Fact on Fruits and Vegetables

Fun Facts on Small Animals

Fun Facts on Dogs for Kids.

Made in United States
North Haven, CT
04 December 2023